The Pains And Gains Of Disappointment

Michael Adikwu

PUBLISHED by PARABLES
Earthly Stories with a Heavenly Meaning

The Pains And Gains Of Disappointment
Michael Adikwu

Published By Parables
June, 2020

All Rights Reserved. No part of this book may be reproduced or utilized in any form or by any means, electronic or mechanical, including photocopying, recording, or by any information storage and retrieval system, without permission in writing from the author.

    ISBN 978-1-951497-71-2
    Printed in the United States of America

Readers should be aware that Internet Web sites offered as citations and/or sources for further information may have been changed or disappeared between the time this was written and the time it is read.

The Pains and Gains Of Disappointment

Michael Adikwu

PUBLISHED by PARABLES
Earthly Stories with a Heavenly Meaning

Table of Content

1.
Various Talks of Disappointment....
7

2.
God's Disappointment with Man....
15

3.
Man's Disappointment with God....
23

4.
The Disappointment of Abraham....
25

5.
The Disappointment of Isaac....
31

6.
The Disappointment of Jacob....
39

7.
The Disappointment of Joseph....
43

8.
The Disappointment of Naomi and Ruth....
477

9.
The Disappointment of Moses....
53

10.
The Disappointment of the Prophets..
57

11.
The Disappointment of Jesus....
63

12.
The Gains of Disappointment....
67

13.
Disappointment and the Desert Life....
69

14.
Disappointment and Prayer Life....
71

15.
Gains of Disappointments that Lead to Death....
75

Preface

Every thoughtful man knows that to achieve anything in life there must be some level of dependence on one person or the other. The dynamics of the society is to try to achieve a balance between relationships so as to avoid the hurtful aspects as much as possible in human existence. When this balance is displaced in favour of another to a point where there is an ill-feeling on the part of one person or group of persons, then there is said to be a disappointment.

Many people become crest-fallen when they encounter disappointment. Many at times it has lead to chronic diseases, stress, and even death. Have you ever met a man complaining of discomfort to the extent of going to the hospital and yet nothing is diagnosed. Some may complain of internal heat, loss of appetite, insomnia and so many other diseases and ailments have come from disappointment. In all men link disappoint as bad behaviour from other individuals. Not too many people link disappointment with what may actually lead to growth both physically and spiritually. After all, it is in the human mind to always think of good and never of evil towards himself or herself. We never even think that we have been sources of disappointment to others. God thinks differently. We need disappointment in many cases to be able to fit into God's plan for our lives.

The first eleven chapters talked about various aspects of disappointment including man's disappointment with fellow human beings. These chapters also highlight man's disappointment with his Creator and the Creator's disappointment with his creatures. Be it the prophets or Jesus Himself, there has been some level of disappointment or the other. The remaining chapters concentrate on the gains of disappointment. Apart from the gains, on the earth while we are still alive, disappointment can gain for us eternal life as well as result in the conversion of others. That is the basis for this book.

M. U. Adikwu,
Abuja, 2014

Acknowledgement

I sincerely thank the Almighty God for giving me the opportunity to write this book. Many would want to write a religious book but are unable to do so. I wish to sincerely thank my beloved wife Victoria who has always occupied in my absence. She has always been on duty taking care of the children in my absence. I am highly indebted to my three youngest children Abraham, Enoch and Abigail, who have missed me the most while away serving the government on an education project. I am also most grateful to all those who have brought disappointment to my life in one way or the other. No man can give a genuine account of what he has not experienced. God allows us to have disappointments so that we can use that to comfort others. Apostle Paul in the Bible will simply say,

"Praise be to the God and Father of our LORD Jesus Christ, the Father of compassion and the God of all comfort, who comforts us in all our troubles, so that we can comfort those in any trouble with the comfort we ourselves have received from God. For just as the sufferings of Christ flows into our lives, so also through Christ our comfort overflows. If we are distressed, it is for your comfort and salvation; if we are comforted, it is for your comfort which produces in you patient endurance of the same sufferings we suffer. And our hope for you is firm, because we know that as you share in our sufferings, so also you share in our comfort."

I am also grateful to the persons who wrote the Internet articles that some aspects were used in the last chapter on the martyrs of the early Christians. May the good LORD reward all of them abundantly.

Chapter 1
Introduction - Various Talks of Disappointments

Day after day we hear of disappointments. Disappointment seems to be part and parcel of human existence on earth. I am sure God Himself is disappointed with human beings and their activities on earth. We hear of children who have disappointed their parents and vice-versa. There are also stories of woes of disappointment between husbands and wives; between lovers; between apprentices and their masters. In fact, it is not a common phenomenon for a man to satisfy another. The failure to satisfy ends in disappointment.

Common Disappointments

In the early parts of past few centuries, it seemed that men were more than women. Getting married then was a difficult phenomenon. This was due largely not to cost of marriage, but to the scarcity of women. Many men then would "secure" females early from a neighbour's house, either for themselves or their male children. The man or family concerned would approach the neighbour with some money to "deposit on the head" of the girl when the girl is still very tender in age. Such girls are often sent some gifts from time to time to enable them to 'grow up properly.' When such girls become mature enough to be married, many would refuse to get married to the person that has "deposited the money on their heads." Such disappointments are usually very painful, because the man might have waited for a prolonged period of time, sometimes up to 10 years or more. The man might have sent the girl to school to acquire

Western education at his own expense. The girls or their families might on the long run refuse the girls to get married to such men for very flimsy reasons. It is possible that the girls have seen richer men than the first or the girls suddenly realize on growing up that the men were not 'clean' enough or even that they are more educated than the men. Quarrels too between the two families concerned may result to the termination of the relationships or the men may finally find out that the girl is not well behaved. In more recent times, this is not too common because most people will only marry girls that are matured. What exists now is that some women, because of advancing age, may get themselves betrothed to a young man and train them in schools. After completion of their trainings, many of such young men refuse to be joined to the women in marriage because of their advanced age, thus disappointing the women. Some of these boys may have entered one form of covenant or the other with the women. This, however, does not deter them from marrying other women on the long run.

There are also disappointments between wives and their husbands. Some wives do everything to keep their husbands happy. They are good looking as far as the human eyes are concerned. Yet some of these husbands go after other women and lavish their love on them instead of their legally married wives. Many of these women are disappointed in their husbands, wondering, "What do these other women have that I do not have?" They wonder if these were not the same men who promised heaven and earth when they first came to them. They have forgotten that it is the pattern of men to serve good wine first and the bad later (John 2:10). It is only God that does the opposite. The disappointment becomes more serious if the husband comes home with a sexually transmitted disease.

Similarly, some men are disappointed with their wives. When they first went to marry them, anything was good when they first met their men. Now that they are in their husbands' houses, nothing is good. The husband may do all in their power to please their wives but such wives are never satisfied. They demand for one thing after the other. They must be given Hollandaise or nothing more. They eat the best and choicest meals while only the remnant is kept for their husbands. They hate everything about their husbands even the way they laugh.

One of the most painful groups of disappointments are those who come from one's relatives. There are some people who all the days of their lives have worked to train their brothers and sisters. At the end, all these people get as 'thank you' is to be abused and asked how senseless they are. They often reminded of the number of cars their classmates have bought; the numbers of houses their classmates have built both in the village and in the cities. Their wives are often regarded as the major devourer that have "eaten-up" all that such men have laboured for, even when their wives may have starved to ensure that such men train their relatives. Many of such men and their wives end up being highly disappointed in life.

There is also the issue of fathers who have laboured all of their lives and have "achieved very little" in the eyes of the world because of taking care of their wives and children. Many of such men end up being disappointed when on the long run their wives and children tag them non-achievers. I remember that one of such men told me one day that he would prefer to kill his wife and face the law instead of his wife's continuous nagging that he has not been able to buy a car as his other colleagues had done. I thank God that this man eventually did not kill his wife before his death. He, however, was able to buy a car from bank loans. Probably the nagging worked. The pains from such nagging wives about one's ineptitude can be very serious, especially when one notices that such women are usually very demanding with very little to show from their own end. I am sure a few husbands might have ended up killing their wives. Others might have committed suicide, while worst still, some might have ended up exterminating their entire family through killing their wives, children and themselves.

There are also cases of disappointments between apprentices and their masters. These disappointments between masters and servants are common especially in business dealings. Some people hire others to sell for them for some fixed period of time under an agreement that after the stated period they will "settle" them. "Settle" as used here means their masters will in turn provide the money, and sometimes introduce them to big companies that may provide some wares or goods on hire-purchase to the new business men. For some the amount of money agreed upon is quite small as their masters know they will introduce them to various ways of doing business including introducing them to big firms that are ready to supply the goods "free" until the emergent business man is well settled to be able to make returns. Many of the apprentices serving such masters become disappointed as some masters may refuse to "settle" them at the end of the agreed period, as they may see the new business entrants as competitors. This has led to great disappointments. Some people have ended up in killing their masters in such cases and vice versa. The situation is most pathetic when such masters have used their apprentices, not only as business associates but as housemaids as well. This is more common with traders than other forms of apprentice relationship such as carpentry, tailoring, mechanics, etc. In these other forms of servant-master relationship only the knowledge acquired is considered most of the time and the apprentice may have to pay for this.

Another area of common disappointment is found when men pool together their resources to start a business. As the business grows one of the partners often try to outwit the other in money sharing. Some even try to seek to stop one of the partners from continuing with the business through the use of legal means while others may use brute force including diabolic means. The partner being cheated out of the business often feels disappointed.

Hired labourers often disappoint those who hire them. In many village settings, labourers are hired for farm work. Most of such labourers require payment of the entire money or part of it upfront. Many at times, the labourers end up not doing the work they have been paid to do. Many of such hired labourers are good at disappointing those who hired them. On the long run the person concerned may look for other labourers who may repeat what their predecessors have earlier done.

Another group of disappointers are the artisans – such as tailors, carpenters, cobblers, bricklayers, e.t.c. Often this group of workers will collect a job to be done but rarely keep to the terms of the agreement in terms of timing. For example, a carpenter may agree to produce some pieces of furniture at an agreed price within two weeks. At the end of two months and in some cases, 2 years, the said pieces of furniture are yet to be produced, even when some or all of the money has been paid for the said furniture. The artisans may prefer to collect other new jobs even when they have not completed the old one. The clients are often very disappointed.

There is what is often referred to as "contribution" – a kind of thrift society. Many people cannot do much with their monthly salaries especially when it comes to capital-intensive projects such as building a house, buying a new car or even marrying a wife. Some are not even able to pay the school fees of their children. With these, many workers or even business men come together to agree on how to raise large sums of money without interest. Thus, there is an agreement that each member of the "contribution" group should set aside some amount to be paid at periodic levels to a member of the group. This is usually on a rotary basis. Some members, once they get their turn of money refuse to pay for others leading to a great disappointment among other members.

And yet still some other people approach wealthier friends or neighbours or even those at the same social level as they are who may have some money to spare and borrow such money from them. The neighbour or friend may even have need for such money but may believe that the borrower may have more urgent need. At the end of the agreed period many people do refuse to return the money lent to them even when they have it. This is often a common disappointment to friends and neighbours.

There are various levels of disappointment in our society. Many parents are very disappointed in their children when they find out that their children belong to secret cults or even armed robbery gangs. Many of such parents may be providing more money than their children may need only to find out that they are indirectly contributing to the purse of secret cults. Great is usually the disappointment when news reaches them that their children belong to one clandestine group or the other. Similarly many Christians become extremely disappointed when they realize that their pastors whom they have held so high are members of secret cults or robbers or even womanizers or rapists. A loving family wakes up one day to note that the man of the house has impregnated her maid or that the house help has impregnated her mistress. What a disappointment this could be! Thus it seems that human existence is replete with disappointments

Michael Adikwu

CHAPTER TWO
GOD'S DISAPPOINTMENT WITH MAN

For a man that is wealthy, possessing a lot of money and all that is required in life to have a beggarly child who lives as a poor wretch is usually a heartache for the parents. If that makes meaning to the reader, then we should note that no rich man is comparable to the All-rich, All-powerful God. All the things you see on earth are actually below what God can do. That is because what we are seeing are actually the shadow of the reality. A man with perfect relationship with God and has seen heaven where Truth and Reality have their origin, he will be able to say that all I am trying to put down are actually understatements. If that is how rich and powerful our God is, why are we disappointing God by failing to use these provisions? What a disappointment we are to Him. In some cultures in Nigeria, people have killed their relatives who went mad because he is seen as a disappointment to the family. Others have killed their children who changed religion because of disappointment. Others have been chased away from home for living below the expectations of their rich parents. Many of the stories of saints who came from rich homes, showed that they were seriously humiliated for rejecting richness and embracing poverty. Even for us as individuals today, many of us take the vow of poverty but never live any life of deprivation. At least, it is an abuse to our status, we think!

When God created man, His intentions for man have never been imagined and will never be imagined. All that we were told is that everything in the Garden of Eden, he should freely eat (Genesis 3:16). Yes everything man needed was available to him. The Garden of Eden God made for man was indescribable because it had a river with four branches. For many of us, building a personal house with a swimming pool is usually the talk of the town. For this Garden, it had four pools! (Genesis 2:10-14). Not only the river but the land surrounding the river was endowed with all forms of precious stones!

Adam did not pay dowry before marriage. It seems that those things we work for these days and boast of as achievements are actually meant to be free. How pitiable a father will see his child when the father buys a car free-of-charge for his son, and the son says, "Thank you sir, but I must work for it!" In the same vein, if a father builds a good house for his son, and he decides to live in a rented house, where he has to work and look for the money, his father will be very disappointed.

One may ask me, why God decided to place any law at all for man not eat the tree at the centre of the Garden (Genesis 2:17). No matter how wealthy a father is, does he not put some restraints on his son so that the son can depend on him and grow up properly. Is there any father who because of love and wealth will tell his son to behave any how? And that the son can set cars and houses ablaze and even lie with the mother? If all these are allowed, then who is in charge? The forbidden fruit was only a tree of dependence upon God. Immediately man ate that three he became independent of God. Any man that is fully dependent upon God has no limitations while anyone who is independent of God is completely finished. Once man fell he became a selfish being. The man that God had formed He intended to participate in His divine nature since he actually possessed this nature. There was to be perfect unity among humans as there was and still exists in the God-head, the Trinity. The new nature man acquired from the devil was opposed to this. Thus in Genesis 3: 8-10 the Bible records:

"And they heard the voice of the Lord God walking in the garden in the cool of the day: and Adam and his wife hid themselves from the presence of the Lord God among the trees of the garden. And the Lord God called unto Adam, and said unto him, where art thou? And he said, I heard thy voice in the garden, and I was afraid, because I was naked; and I hid myself."

Remember that most things that lead a man to hiding are sinful. No man will want to do something lawful and then decides to hide. In fact, the action of hiding is itself a separation. Hiding is simply saying, "Darkness, cover me." Hiding from God is seeking refuge in Darkness. God is light and once we hide from His source of light, we give ourselves to the devil, the source of darkness. One of the greatest disappointments God had with man is this loss of fellowship with him and giving ourselves freely to the devil. God is a God of fellowship. Just as a lover likes to stay with his loved one, so also God likes to fellowship and remain with him. He wants us primarily to remain close to him. The attitude shown by Adam in the above statement shows a great level of separation, not only from God, but also from his wife. Do you wonder then why man finds it difficult to stay at peace with his wife? He used 4 "I$_s$" as if here were alone. It seems that Adam forgot that he was with his wife. He spoke to defend himself and not the woman with him.

The Lord God who likes fellowship called Moses to the Mountain thus: ***"Come up to me into the mount and be there ....."*** When Moses went up to meet the Lord, he was there, covered in the cloud, for six good days (Exod. 24:15-16). It was only the seventh day that the Lord began to speak and to instruct him about the Ten Commandments. For six days, the Lord was just having personal fellowship with him. In Mark 3: 14, we are told Jesus ordained twelve that they **should** be with Him and that He **might** send them forth to preach. The purpose of Jesus ordaining the twelve was primarily that "they should be_with Him." The issue of sending them forth to preach was secondary as the Bible used the word "**might.**" Fellowship is a primary call of God upon our lives. In Luke 10: 38-42, we are told of the story of the visitation of Jesus to the house of Mary and Martha. Martha was busy cooking for Jesus and his disciples while Mary sat fellowshipping with Jesus. When Martha approached Jesus to release her sister Mary for the Kitchen work His reply was simply, ***"Martha, Martha, thou are worried and troubled about many things: But one thing is needful and Mary has chosen that good part, which shall not be taken away from her."*** Staying with Jesus and thus fellowshipping with Him is superior to even food. Many people, including those working in the Lord's vineyard are today performing below expectation because of lack of proper quality time with God. Many are too troubled about many things and as such cannot take enough time out to pray. God is, as such, disappointed with our performances. Even in our secular jobs, many of us are performing below the expectations of Heaven.

The Issue of Greed and Selfishness

Heaven expected perfect unity and love among men where everyone makes contribution to his neighbor's existence on earth. Unfortunately this was thwarted by the fall. God is therefore seriously disappointed in man pertaining particularly to his greed and selfishness. When the Lord God called Adam in the Garden of Eden, look at his answer once more, "I heard thy voice in the garden, and I was afraid, because I was naked and I hid myself." Genesis 3: 10. This answer presupposes that Adam was alone. Everything was "I". That is the life of fallen man. Everything is about himself. Adam must have hidden with his wife in the same place, yet he never recognized her presence. I expected Adam to have said, "we heard thy vice in the garden, and we were afraid, because we were naked and we hid ourselves." This was however, not the case. Do you then wonder that Adam had to give a name to the woman God gave him? She was simply "woman" in Genesis 2:23 because she was the bone of his bones and flesh. Adam simply said, **"She shall be called woman because she was taken out of man."** After the fall, this idea completely changed. The story became, **"And Adam called his wife's name Eve because she was the mother of all living."** There was a change from "bone of my bones" to "mother of all living." To the man, the woman simply became the producer of children. The woman was being simply told, "Your duty from today onwards is to produce." Do you then wonder why many homes are broken when the woman fails to produce? And these days, woman must not only produce children, she must also produce money. In many countries of the world, women are simply the burden bearers. They must produce and bring up the children; they must produce the food for the family. They must produce the water that the entire family needs. They must bring home the firewood that the family needs to cook its food.

Those that call their names darling, honey, my own, e.t.c, do they know that none is as wonderful as simply calling her "woman"? Each time you call your wife "woman", you are simply calling her "bone of my bones and flesh of my flesh." If only we will learn this. It is the height of love any man can give to his wife. It is a name that brings unity. Do you know that in the Bible Jesus often referred to His mother as "woman"? He saw and recognized the power and beauty in this name, woman. In John 2:4, the Bible says, "Jesus said unto her, **"Woman what have I to do with thee? My hour has not yet come."** Again, on the cross, **"When Jesus therefore saw His Mother and the disciples standing by, whom He loved, He said unto His mother, Woman behold thy son."** Even after the resurrection, when He saw Mary of Magdala standing and weeping by His tomb, the angels never addressed her by her name. They simply said, **"Woman why weepest thou?"** John 20:13 Jesus also called her first, **"Woman why weepest thou, whom seekest thou?"** It was the failure of Mary to recognize Jesus (John 20:14) that made Jesus to call her "Mary" probably in a tune that will enable Mary to recognize Him. Woman is the heavenly name given to women by the glorious un-fallen man. The names we give our female children today are part of the greed and selfishness that heaven is lamenting about. Many give some names to show how religious we are or to show that is the most beautiful and unique name in town. You may even see idol worshippers calling their children "Agatha"! What hypocrisy! The beauty of a woman is her character that reflects the "bone of my bones' and not how sweet the name is in the cheeks.

Immediately after the Pentecost experience, the Bible records that all the disciples were together and had all things common (Acts 2:44). This is the plan of heaven. God wants us to see all things as common so that we can possess it without pride or selfish ambition. Do you know the greatest disappointment of God with man today? It is the spirit of competition among them. Every man wants to ride the best car in town, or build the best house in the city. If he is given the opportunity, he will prevent others from buying such cars or building such houses. This is why there is no peace upon the surface of the earth.

A man is ready to go to any length so as to be praised and thought superior to others. Many sacrifice their wives and children. Others bury people alive just to win a political contest. Others see other races as inferior. Many species of human beings eat other species. A friend told me that the name cannibal is because of some human eaters who sacrificed their children to the Phoenician god called Baal. The name cannibal, therefore, originated from "Canaan Baals." Whether this is true or not, the same practice is here with us and is even worsening as men approach the devil for power through various sacrifices. I do not see this abating because he is as true as he was during creation and the deceit of Adam and Eve. Every Christian must be on guard not to disappoint God. Going to the devil is like leaving a Father who has all things and going to another who has nothing. For this reason, God was very disappointed with the Israelites for leaving Him to choose different useless gods who brought only misery and disaster to them. Unfortunately, many of us, like the Israelites have chosen this path of misery in the name of earthly possession in pursuit of fame and wealth which are the trade marks of the devil. Do you know what the devil said to Jesus? **"All these things, will I give thee, if thou will fall down and worship me."** This desire of the defeated devil has not changed. Once you want a piece of the earth, you must fall down and worship the devil unless God is the one giving you a piece of that earth. Thus many wicked men who have died may even have streets named after them because they actually fell down and worshipped the devil. The story in the Old Testament clearly shows how God was disappointed with the Israelites. He sent them Judges and Prophets to correct them but to no avail. Shall we continue to disappoint God as they did? Remember that they did not have the opportunity that we have of experiencing Jesus. Jesus would tell his listeners that if Sodom and Gomorrah had heard the message we are hearing, they would have repented. May God help us in this matter, because in all generations men have disappointed Him but He has always had a remnant? In the generation of Adam, Abel was the remnant that pleased God. In the generations that followed, we could talk about Enoch, Noah, Abraham, Moses, Joshua, Caleb, e.t.c.

Won't you want to be among those that will not disappoint God? Men who did not disappoint God had one thing in common. They were a disappointment to the people of their time. Are you too busy with trying to make yourself famous and as such make a name for yourself? Certainly you will be a disappointment to God. Men who did not disappoint God were not popular. Why their names seem popular is because the Holy Ghost wanted their names to be brought to the fore. I do not think Abel was popular, neither was Enoch. Similarly neither Noah nor Abraham was popular. At best they were "mad men" who "hear spirits" to their generation. Will you want to be counted as a madman for God?

CHAPTER 3
MAN'S DISAPPOINTMENT WITH GOD

There are times whereby it is actually man that is disappointed with God. Why does God not act when He is supposed to? Why is there so much suffering in the world? Why should the good man suffer at all? At most times, it is even the ungodly that even suffers less. This is a question that even the Psalmist had to ask (Psalm 73). Some people are so disappointed with life events that they even "remain restless" in their graves or do I say men think that they remain restless in their graves? No wonder people talk about 'rest in peace' (RIP) when a man dies. Or Do I say that those alive plead with them to remain in peace?

Many psychosomatic disorders are due to these disappointments in life especially when men think that God should intervene and He does not seem to do so. Many have died from such ailments while others have committed suicide. Many of the suicide cases we hear about in advanced countries are disappointment-related. It may be nice to look at some examples where man thinks God may be responsible or should have intervened in certain disasters.

A newly-wedded couple went on a honey moon only for one of the couples to get drowned. Another set of newly-weds perished in a plane crash. We hear of people who after defending their PhD thesis die in auto crashes the same week or even a few weeks later. Others are taken away by what is often referred to as "brief illnesses' after an excellent achievement in life. It is also a common occurrence that the only boy of a family is taken away by the cold hands of death just before his 20th birth day. Worst still the only child of a family is snatched away by the cold hands of death at an early age leaving the couple childless. There are also cases where an entire family perishes in one disaster or the other leaving no memory of them at all. A man who has never made love to any woman but in his first attempt he contracts one deadly disease while another who has been a womanizer from his youth has no such experiences. A well-loved football team that has also played very well loses a football match which clearly should have been to their favour. In a nation where religion is very popular, members of one religion wonder why God allows infidels to come to power through elections and other means. A pastor, while preaching in a church, collapses and dies. Many just people are punished unjustly while the unjust grow from strength to strength winning different accolades and titles in the society. A man who steals a goat is jailed for six months while another who steals billions of Naira or Dollars because he is working in a public office is jailed for two weeks at the end of which his people or admirers welcome him with fanfare. A man kills another man and is hanged after much torture in detention. Another man leads his nation to war leading to the death of millions and at the end he becomes a hero with streets named after him. A couple who never messed-up sexually while they were young end up having difficulty in bearing children after wedding while prostitutes plead for heaven to stop them from having more than 10 children after marriage! The question every man will ask about all these is, "Does God exist?" Those who believe in His existence become very disappointed with him. No wonder Job's wife could tell his husband to curse God and die (Job 2: 8-10). To her, God has become a disappointment.

CHAPTER 4
THE DISAPPOINTMENTS OF ABRAHAM

Abraham in the Bible is called the father of the faithful. How did he arrive at this title? Was it smooth for him all through life? Did he meet with disappointments?

Abraham's family was one that seemed to have walked with God. It seemed that the message to leave his father's house to go to Canaan had first come to Abraham's father although this is not very clear in the Bible. In Genesis 11:31 we are told, that, **"Tera took his son Abram, his grandson Lot son of Haran, and his daughter-in-law Sarai, the wife of his son Abram, and together they set out from Ur of the Chaldees to go to Canaan. But when they came to Haran, they settled there."**

Thus the journey to Canaan started with Abraham's father, Tera. It should, however, be noted that the final journey which we are popularly familiar with came after the death of Tera. More noteworthy is the introductory sentence in Genesis 12, **"The Lord had said to Abram, Leave your country, your people and your father's household and go to the land I will show you."**

Take a second look on the **Lord had** said to Abram......." This means it was actually in Genesis 11 that God spoke to Abraham; and as mentioned probably to his father too. Abraham did not leave Ur of the Chaldees to go to Canaan; it was his father who did. Abraham obeyed this call and left Haran to go to Canaan after his father's death and left with his nephew Lot, who had become his liability through the action of his father.

On this journey of faith, Abraham had some disappointments both from God and his nephew Lot.

Abraham pitched his tent in Bethel (Genesis 12:8). It seems that before long there was famine in the land and Abraham went down to Egypt to live there for a while because the famine was severe (Genesis 12:10). Many may accuse Abraham for going to Egypt without first of all praying and asking God. Supposing he prayed and God did not answer probably because it was His design to let Him go to Egypt? Most great men in the Bible visited Egypt one time or the other. We should also remember that most of that time God visited Abraham were not because he prayed. In fact he built altars only after God visited him.

We should also remember that walking with God does not mean that we discuss with God at will. No. He chooses the time and the seasons to visit us. There are people who pray that anytime they ask God for anything He would talk to them. That would be wonderful but it is often not so. Even for the prophets in the Old Testament, the seasons, the times and the month were often recorded. This means that God does not at all times talk to even the prophets. Sometimes they had to wear ephods before God could speak. I am sure Abraham had some disappointments in this direction as we do today. While he was in Egypt, he had to tell a lie that Sarai was not his wife (Genesis 12:20). If God had prevented him from going to Egypt through abundant supply, this would not have befallen him.

Abraham left Egypt and went back to Bethel (Genesis 13:1). There he prayed and called on the name of the LORD. By this time Lot, his brother's son, had had an increase in his possession of herds and flocks and tents and as such the land they stayed together because of the large number of their possessions (Genesis 13:5-6).

Quarrelling arose between Abraham's herdsmen and those of Lot (Genesis 13:7). This must have been a great disappointment to Abraham. His own nephew has grown big to challenge him. After all, his prosperity came because God was with Abraham. At this point separation was inevitable.

Abraham had to call a peace meeting between him and his nephew (Genesis 13:8). Abraham requested that Lot should give him any portion of the land that was pleasing to him. What a Godly man. He did not choose first. In his greed, **"Lot looked up and saw that the whole plain of the Jordan was well watered, like the garden of the Lord, like the Land of Egypt, toward Zoar"** (Genesis 13:10). The poor boy would have told him, **"You chose first, sir."**

Lot decided to choose first because he could see green grass for his cattle. He did not know that it was the direction of Sodom and Gomorrah. He did not know that he was going to live among wicked people that the Lord had earmarked for destruction. God spoke to Abraham again after Lot had departed (Genesis 13:14). There are some relatives that may be obstacles to our walk with God.

Before long, war broke out and Lot and his family and his possessions were taken away (Genesis 14). Does that sound funny? Many of our choices in life that are based on human feelings can only lead us to trouble. How disappointed Abraham must have been with this nephew. Yet he went and rescued him from the hands of his captors. What a godly man Abraham was. No wander he is referred to as the father of the faithful. In all these Abraham had not had a child. He had to express his disappointment openly to God at a particular time.

"O Sovereign Lord, what can you give me since I remain childless and the one who will inherit my estate is Eliezer of Damascus. You have given me no children, so a servant in my house will be my heir."

Thank God, Abraham still referred to God as **sovereign LORD**. To some people in that situation, the LORD would no longer be sovereign. They will simply say, "This has passed issue for prayers" thus belittling God. In his disappointment Abraham still had hope. Do you have bad relatives? They can be rescued. Are you disappointed in God? He is still sovereign and will answer you at the appointed time.

The next disappointment Abraham had was with his wife. In Genesis 16:1 we are told that Sarah told Abraham, *"The Lord has kept me from having children. Go Sleep with my maidservant; perhaps I can build my family through her."*

And so Abraham slept with Hagar, the Egyptian maiden of Sarah and she became pregnant. Before we continue to look at the disappointments of Abraham, let's take a look at the statement of Sarah above. *"The LORD has kept me from having children."* For Sarah it was the LORD. She recognized the sovereignty of the LORD. She did not attribute her problems to Abraham's father's idolatry. She did not associate her problem with one demon or the other. She did not attribute her problems to the "inability of her husband to perform." She did not attribute her problems to the witches and wizards of Canaan. It was the LORD! The LORD is sovereign above all principalities, powers and authority. If only we can view all our problems like that, it will be wonderful. In our generation all our problems are due to one demon, man or woman. These are strange doctrines.

Then, as typical of women, once Hagar conceived and began to despise her mistress, the problem was placed on the head of Abraham. "You are responsible for the wrong I am suffering. I put my servant in your arms, and now that she knows she is pregnant, she despises me. May the LORD judge between you and me."

I am sure Abraham was disappointed with his wife. Abraham never told Hagar to despise her mistress. Yet, she is referred to as the root cause of her wife's problems. That is the nature of man; always looking for where to put the blame. And so the disappointments of Abraham continued. Abraham was 86 years when Hagar bore Ishmael. God visited him again when he was 99 years (Genesis 16:16; Genesis 17:1). This was almost 13 years gap. You could imagine a man like Abraham not having fellowship with God for 12 years! Sarah did not look at the damage she had caused to the relationship between God and Abraham. Instead, she was more concerned with the disobedience of her slave girl. Meanwhile a covenant that will affect generations was at stake if Abraham had behaved like the men of our time. He might have decided to send Sarah away now that there was a productive little girl in his house. Thank God that he did not do that. From this point onwards, God kept confirming his covenant of Abraham's own child through Sarah. Year after year his hope continued to be shaken while his confusion continued to increase.

I am sure Abraham's disappointment with himself increased when his wife died, some years after he has gotten Isaac. A man that was entitled to the inheritance of his father's land had to buy a portion of land from the Hittites (Genesis 23). Does this speak to you? It may come to a point that a man who is comfortable in his home is moved away to a different place either on assignment or as a missionary. The comfort he has enjoyed before becomes illusive as he has to look for a new accommodation which may not be available. He has to learn to live in huts in some cases and many at times he has to adjust to new climate, new diet, new friends, e.t.c. Finally, Abraham never inherited any land before his death! What a disappointment. The Bible only recorded that he died holding onto the promises (Hebrews 11:13). One thing was, however, clear. He saw the promises afar off with the eyes of faith. He and his descendants admitted that they were aliens and strangers on earth. How I wish we can think like this! It is one sure way of putting off every problem we encounter.

CHAPTER 5
THE DISAPPOINTMENTS OF MOSES

Moses was someone whose problems began at birth. Like many other Israelite children of his time, his birth was at a time when the nation was in a strange land in Egypt with all the attendant difficulties. The Bible recorded that Pharaoh had directed that all the male children born of the Hebrews should be cast into the river. Does this seem harsh to you? It is at the same level of what is called birth control today. Some of these designs are from the pit of hell. Many things that became popular are actually from the pit of hell.

By divine providence, however, Moses was saved. The story of Moses that is recorded in Exodus Chapter 1 clearly shows that God's hand was involved in the salvation of Moses from the cruel Egyptians. I will not retell the story here because it is a well known story even to non-Christians. All that is important is that Moses was spared because there was a duty that God had destined him to do. God sees the end from the beginning and thus the Bible recorded that when the mother beheld him, he was a fine child (Exodus 2:2). I begin to wander how many mothers will see their new-born babies and declare that "this is not a fine child!" All children are born fine, at least in the eyes of the parents. Even for malformed children, it is a struggle to declare that "this child is not fine." This issue of fine child connotes more than we can put down here, since I am not just writing an essay on Moses.

The truth is that the mother tried to keep her 3 months unnoticed. This also connotes that God was in the matter. How could one keep a baby for three months! The neighbours must know. If the Egyptians did not know, at least the Hebrew neighbours who have lost their children must know and the consequence of being reported was possible. Finally the child was placed in a reed near the bank of a river. God protected the baby and coincidentally brought Pharaoh's daughter to the river. Whatever gave her a good heart towards the child must again be God. After all she knew earlier that children were being thrown into the river.

This story is not peculiar to Moses. It is for all us. There have been "Pharaohs" around who have declared that we must not live. That is why many have died at birth. These "Pharaohs" may even be unseen. We have also had neighbours whose children died at birth while our mothers were carrying us alive. They must have reported us to "their authorities" but today, like Moses, we are alive. Our mothers have helplessly placed us on "reeds" and kept "our sisters" nearby and "Pharaoh's daughters" have come to our rescue. Many of the sicknesses, be it malaria, measles, diarrhea, typhoid, e.t.c. we suffered at infancy are all these "reeds" that show how helpless our mothers were. Yet God sent our "sisters" and the "Pharaoh's" daughters in the form of drugs and nurses and doctors and even praying pastors and parents. All these may not be important, except that God has seen that we are "fine" and that there is a job for us to do. How foolish then if we think that all that God has done to keep us alive is just for us to lavish everything we have on our lusts.

And so Moses grew partly in the hands of his own mother and largely under the hands of Pharaoh's daughter, and even became an heir designate (Acts. 7:21, Hebrews 11:24). It seems that through "divine" instruction he knew that he was not an Egyptian. Through the same divine instruction Moses had thought he would be the leader of his people. The Bible recorded that "It came into his heart" to visit his brethren the Israelites (Acts 7:23). I am sure that was the last visitation before he ran into exile. I am sure this was almost a political visit- a kind of campaign visit. Moses thought that his own people would realize that God was using him to rescue them, but they did not (Acts. 7:25). He killed an Egyptian who was fighting with a Hebrew. At another period, it was two Hebrew men that were at loggerheads. He tried to make peace but it turned out that his peace mission was not acceptable to them. The Israelite who was maltreating the other simply told him, **"Who made you a ruler and judge over us?"** (Acts 7:27). I am sure he was disappointed with himself for his actions – first for visiting his people from the heart of Egypt and secondly for killing the Egyptian. I am also sure that he was disappointed with his own people and with God. Will his own people not understand that with all their suffering they should simply accept him and be rescued from their tormentors? Why had God "told" him this if He would not make his people to obey him? In the confusion that ensued Moses ran to Midian. I do not know what God has told you or what you feel you want to become in life? For every divine appointment there is an appointed time. God made you for a purpose but you must fit into His timetable. Do not rush into what you think you want to do for God! The bad news is that He does not want you to do anything for Him. He knows how to do things for Himself. He only will use you as a channel at the appointed time. You are only an instrument in God's hand. A man may buy a cutlass and even sharpen it but the cutlass must not go on its own to cut grass. It may cut in the enemies' field. It may cut where the owner wants to spare and get grass for a different purpose! You should only be a ready vessel in God's hands. That was the problem with Moses. His people were suffering. If he did not act when God had not told him, his people's suffering might have been shortened. He prolonged his people's suffering for another 40 years. Many of you are saying that people are dying and going to hell, so you want to act fast. The situation has been so before you were born. It has not gotten out of hand because God is in control. He is always sovereign. He knows what to do. His hour is not your hour. When God gives you appointment, He knows when you should assume duties. Do not allow your human energy to push you into going before God. He should be in front while you follow. What made Moses to commit these errors was his human energy or youthful exuberance. At 40 he was at the peak and thought it was time to become the president of his people. He had to dissipate this energy before God could use him. How do I know this? His reply when he finally met God in the desert indicated very clearly that it was not the "same" Moses that ran away that met God at the end of 40 years after keeping Jethro's sheep. **"Who am I that should go to Pharaoh and bring the Israelites out of Egypt**? This is like the common Nigerian expression, "Me like this!" He started looking at himself from a derogatory point of view. Moses has been sifted of his energy. There was a different "Moses" in Moses.

Many of our people fail today either in the religious life or in political or public offices because they go in with their human energy. That is why men question their authority. Remember that for 40 years Moses had been running after sheep that must be tolerated because they do not have human reasoning. He had learnt patience. Do you know that this sheep must be handled with utmost care unlike other forms of shepherding because they were his in-law's property? One shepherding for his in-law must be extra-careful because any damage to the animals could mean a threat of losing one's wife. Not only this. Moses was living in his in-law's house and was being fed and discipled by him. This is an additional burden as any carelessness act could mean much. This taught Moses humility. It also taught him much care and watchfulness! Do you wonder why God had to call twice, "Moses, Moses" to get his attention? Moses had become an instrument God could use. He had joined the league of men that God could use. He had become prayerful through loneliness and the desire to be careful with his in-law's property. No wonder, God made him a president without any campaign. He faced so many disappointments during the actual leading of the Israelites but we will deal with those in the periphery.

Apart from the personal issues we have raised about Moses, his leadership of the children of Israel resulted in more disappointments. A good case was the family quarrel that resulted between his elder sister, Miriam; his elder brother, Aaron and himself. This was a result of the Ethiopian woman that Moses had married (Numbers 12). Does this sound a bell to those who are married? One of the greatest problems that people who live in extended family practice face is the issue of quarrels resulting between the husband's relatives and his wife or even the man and his brother. An issue must be raised, no matter how good the man is to his relatives or no matter how the wife tries to please the relatives of the husband. It is either the wife is too dirty and does not keep the house clean, or the wife is too "clean" as she is wasting the entire family money on clothes or perfumes. It is either the wife does not like greeting people or she greets too much and must be a talkative. Or is either the wife is too disrespectful and will soon be involved in adultery, if not carefully watched. It is either the wife does not cook for her husband's relatives or she cooks too much and must be chased away for being too extravagant. The list can go on and on. All I am trying to say is that the relatives of the husband must find a reason why the woman must leave their brother's house. I keep considering where they expect the man to find a wife of their choice. After all, most people who manifest this attitude of never being satisfied with whoever their relatives married have worse characters than the woman in question. And so Moses found himself entangled under this kind of mess. Fortunately, Moses never looked at himself. He never prayed casting or binding the demons in Aaron and Miriam. He looked unto God and God vindicated him. Miriam was afflicted with leprosy to indicate that any person is a potential sinner. Do you see the leprosy (sin) in others? You too are a potential leaper! The evil you are quick in pointing out in others can manifest in you too. Do not therefore boast of your clean ways.

Apart from disappointments from his personal family, Moses had several other disappointments. The example I will use here, apart from several others, were those of the murmurings of the Israelites against God and Moses. Why I have singled this out is that this is the greatest evil that has befallen man today. God spoke with Moses and with the Israelites face to face, yet all that they wanted to depend upon was themselves. At the verge of their entry into the Promised Land Moses sent 12 spies to check out the land.

Ten came back comparing themselves with the Anakites and the Amalekites, e.t.c., that dwelt in the land (Numbers 13 & 14). They quickly forgot that no children of Anak can divide a Red Sea. They began to look at themselves and at Moses instead of God. This is the greatest problem Christianity is facing today. The world is looking for leaders who will renew the face of the earth. The worst leader can renew the face of the earth if the citizens turn to

God and earnestly seek His face (2Chr. 7:14). People are looking for men who will never fail in any way as role models. Congregations are looking at the characters of their pastors, priests and bishops. "Look onto Jesus" is the shout of the Holy Spirit from heaven. He is the author and finisher of our Faith (Heb 12:2). Both heaven and Moses were disappointed with the children of Israel when they depended on what the eyes could see. They left God backstage as many of us do today and are conquered by our situations. Do not be a disappointment to God. Have an appointment with Him.

CHAPTER 6
DISAPPOINTMENTS OF ISAAC

It will be difficult to discuss the issue of disappointments without having to touch the three pillars of Christian Faith and origin, Abraham, Isaac and Jacob. The case of Isaac may not be as glaring as the other two persons but attempts will be made to state his own disappointments that made him to have appointment with God. Every Christian must note that in talking about the God of the Christians, it is practically impossible not to talk about Him as the God of Abraham, Isaac and Jacob. These are our fathers in faith. God introduced Himself to Moses as the God of Abraham, Isaac and Jacob (Exodus 3:6). Other gods may introduce themselves as the god of Abraham, Ishmael and Jacob or the god of Abraham, Isaac and Esau, e.t.c. You will quickly notice that there is a difference somewhere.

Isaac's disappointments may have come from the polygamous nature of his family as well as well as from the sojourn of his father in a strange land. He might also have been disappointed by God because his life was barren for over 20 years. He is also a good example of a person that God Himself arranged a disappointment around his family life. It is noteworthy that many disappointments may arise from the fallen nature of man but for most people that God wants to be great, He arranges disappointments for them. This is because no man that has appointment with men (even if it is with himself) that can have appointment with God.

Early in life God had demanded that Isaac be scarified as a burnt offering unto the LORD (Genesis 22:2). From the

Bible verse: ***"Take now thy only son Isaac whom you love, and get thee into the land of Moriah; and offer him there for a burnt offering upon one of the mountains which I will show you,"*** two reasons can be deduced why God wanted Abraham to sacrifice Isaac. The first is to test the faithfulness of Abraham to God. Thus God may also demand "our Isaac" to test our faithfulness unto Him. Secondly, is to cut the relationship between Abraham and his son. Take your son "whom you love..." Many of us cannot have appointment with God because of our appointment with our children or even our wives. St. Paul will admonish those who are married to live as though they were not married. Nothing should substitute God in our lives. For some, it is the love for fame. I do know that some people who lived in the past generations made names and were very famous. Some did not even allow this to get into their heads. Isaac Newton was a great scientist as well as a good Christian. We hear of people like Albert Einstein, Linus Pauling, e.t.c. Many of them were religious in one form or the other. Most modern day scientists do not even believe in God. When they die, there names are forever forgotten. Today people effortlessly name their children after John, Peter, and all the early apostles because they had appointment with God. For Abraham, his problem was his, love for Isaac. Do you blame him? Who will have a child at that age from a "dead body" and not be proud of him. God had to arrange to break that love. I see Isaac forever saying to himself, "If not God, my father would have killed me." I am sure he was thoroughly disappointed in a father who would want to use his son for sacrifice. This gave him appointment with a God who could save at the last second to die.

Isaac also knew the disappointment that comes when one loses his mother. More so, he was not married when his mother died (Genesis 24:67). To worsen this matter, he was the only son from his mother. He had other children to contend with and he was not the eldest. Ishmael was there to give him all the beating of his life.

It is not a surprise then that Abraham had to separate them before he died (Genesis 25:6). With the death of Abraham and Sarah, the only thing that would have comforted Isaac in a strange land would have been his own children since he was not living with his brothers. Unfortunately his wife Rebecca was barren (Genesis 25:21). It had to become a matter of serious prayer for about 20 years before his wife could conceive. I am sure Isaac must have been seriously disappointed. He had no relatives, no land of his own, being a stranger in Canaan and to worsen it, no children. The best option would have been to take his wife and return to where his father had migrated from. The Bible recorded that he did not do this because he hoped for a better country whose maker is God. He knew he was just a pilgrim on earth. How I mourn for people who run around from country to country in search of the good life. There is no such here on earth. Men like Abraham and his descendants knew there was no such life on earth. They lived in tents (Hebrew 11:13-16). Do you know what? It was not as even though he was comfortable where he was living. He was not even allowed to drink from the wells his father had dug. Once the people of Gerar saw that Isaac was doing well, he became an object of hatred and jealousy (Genesis 26: 15-34). He was pushed from place to place. Anywhere he dug well; the people would refill it and pursue him out of that land. All these did not cause him to return. He believed God. For many of us, we would quickly have returned to the old way of life once conditions became adverse. It is in your adverse condition that God will meet you and show Himself mighty on your behalf. When Isaac reached a point, where he dug well and he was allowed to settle and drink from it, he simply said, **"The LORD has made room for us......"** Many of us will not wait for the LORD to make room for us. We want to make the room for ourselves no matter what it takes. When God has not made a way and you insist, of course, the devil will make one but you must bow down and worship him in one way or the other (Mathew 4:9). Like his father Abraham, Isaac also faced famine and the threat to take away his wife from him. He certainly had his on dose of disappointments.

CHAPTER 7
DISAPPOINTMENT OF JACOB

The story or account of Jacob as given in the Bible is a disappointment to many and I am sure, even to Jacob himself. He was, I believe, disappointed even in himself. How do I know this? By carefully studying his response when he encountered or met with Pharaoh. Pharaoh said to Jacob, "**How old are you?**" His reply was very touching.

"The days of the years of my pilgrimage are an hundred and thirty years. Few and evil have the years of my life been...... " (Genesis 47:7-9). I am sure Jacob said this with a lot of sorrowful memory, "Evil have the years of my life been." He saw himself as a disappointment. He saw that over the years he has hurt others including his own twin brother, Esau. I, however, thank God for men like him. Their godly heritage showed in the truth they spoke. No wonder he was able to fit into the covenant God had made with his grandfather, Abraham. In another place, he pleaded with an angel to bless him (Genesis 32: 24-26).

*"**And Jacob was left alone; and there wrestled a man with him until the breaking of the day. And when he saw that he prevailed not against him, he touched the hollow of his thigh and the hollow of Jacob's thigh was out of joint as he wrestled with him. And he said, I will not let thee go, except thou bless me.**"*

Does that not tell us much about the heart of Jacob? One who had 12 children and 4 wives? He had servants. He had enough property to give out two hundred she-goats, twenty he-goats, twenty rams, thirty female camels, forty cows, twenty female donkeys, and ten foals, all to his brothe, Esau. He must have been extremely wealthy. Yet, to him, these were no blessings. He knew the origin of these things. He cheated his uncle to acquire some of the property. He married two sisters and even acquired their house-helps as wives. He knew many areas of his life were not clean. He knew he was not under any blessing. As such, he cried out to the angel, "I will not let you go unless you bless me." We sing that sentence as a song but we are only careful about the melody of it. We are not careful that it was the heart cry of a repenting sinner! This was a heart cry of a man who was under the conviction and burden of sin to repent because of the presence of God. Many of us will acquire false certificates, false employment after bribes, buy schools for our children, steal money from government or church coffers only to fix a day of thanksgiving and offering unto the LORD. In fact, we might have even given several testimonies.

For Jacob, it was not a matter of rejoicing. It was a matter of repentance and even a matter of "do or die" as we often say. He knew if he missed this opportunity, it might be forever. He might be forever lost. Who knows when God would encounter him in such a manner again? Many of us see such opportunities and treat tehm lightly. We let them slip-off.

Many may be blaming Jacob for his type of life. Meanwhile his name from birth was prophetic – one who will supplant. He must be among what we call today a spirit child. After all they were only two children in the family. They had enough "space" and opportunity to do whatever they wanted. Their mother Rebecca was barren for twenty years after marriage (Genesis 25:21). As such, I am sure the children were treated with utmost care and love as the manner is with such families. However, it seems that God was ordering the step of Jacob for the inheritance as it was very clear to the mother that the "elder shall serve the younger" (Genesis 25:23). God made this very clear to Rebecca that Jacob will be a special child compared to Esau. This may also be a reason why she loved Jacob more than Esau (Genesis 25:28).

No wonder then that Jacob certainly was a spoilt child as was and still is the manner of such children. One thing that we must note about the life Jacob was that he was prayerful after the manner of his grandfather. We are told in the Bible that he built altars. We are not told so of Esau.

The reason why many people will not reach the maximum height God has for them is not because of their today's sins but because they have abandoned God and have refused to repent. You can use many bad terminologies to describe the life of Jacob. He could be called a womanizer. After cheating his brother of his birth-right (he could also be called a cheat) he ran to his uncle's house (Genesis 28). On his way to his uncle's house, he met the beautiful Rachael, his uncle's daughter. His first reaction was to weep (Genesis 29:11). What manner of lust is that? He was certainly a womanizer. Not only that, he married two sisters and freely accepted their housemaids as well. He however, had disappointments from family quarrels resulting from polygamy.

He also had disappointments in Rachael his sweetheart, because she had difficulty in having children. A greater disappointment came when he finally lost her during childbirth on their way to Bethel (Genesis 35: 16, 19). Jacob had disappointments from her neighbours in Shechem (Genesis 34) who raped his daughter Dina. This was followed by a kind of treachery by his children who caused the men of Schechem to be circumcised. While nursing their wounds two of his children killed all the men in the land because their sister was raped. In addition, he was also disappointed when his children tricked him into believing that Joseph was devoured by a wild beast after selling him into slavery. Jacob had a fair share of disappointments in life but what matters most was what he did under such situations. He did not curse the children who were murderers. Today we talk about the 12 tribes of Israel – all the root of Jacob!

CHAPTER 8
THE DISAPPOINTMENTS OF JOSEPH

The disappointments of Joseph and his later success in life can encourage any Christian who is asking today, "Where is God?" Joseph's disappointment started early having lost his mother at a very tender age – during the birth of his only brother Benjamin (Genesis 35:16-19). Joseph was thus left amidst his elder brothers. The more discomforting situation was the fact his father was a polygamist with three remaining wives. The women were actually adversaries to one another and his mother was one of the main sources of trouble in the family before her death (Genesis 29 and 30). This might have resulted from her barrenness (Genesis 29:31). Joseph was, therefore, in a hostile environment. God, will however, use whoever He wants to use. All these ugly circumstances surrounding Joseph's life did not deter God from using him. He was the child of a second wife. He was from a polygamous background. The family was not even a peaceful one. Amidst all these he began to dream dreams. God was quietly visiting him in the vision of the night. He began to see perhaps a far off; his leadership position. At age seventeen, he began his journey to greatness (Genesis 37:2). In fact heaven gave attention to his record before any of his brothers when the generation of his father, Jacob, was named (Genesis 37:2). At this age he had begun to differentiate evil from good. He had seen how evil his brothers were (Genesis 37:2). He had decided to consecrate his life to God. No wonder, that his father loved him, not just because he was the child of his old age. This love from his father contributed to his greatness. If your father is a pagan and he loves you, and blesses you, God will honour his blessings. Once they noticed that he was loved more than them (Genesis 37:3, 4) they (his brothers) began to hate him. This was the beginning of his troubles. Yet God kept visiting him in dreams.

"We were binding sheaves in the field and lo, my sheaf arose and stood upright; and behold your sheaves stood round about it, and made obeisance to my sheaf."

One interesting word was that his sheaf stood "upright." Many people are not able to attract obedience and respect from people because they are not upright. Uprightness brings victory. Uprightness brings people to respect us even when we are not asking for it. The people of the world want to force people to respect them either through coercion or through achievements. That is why we have walked very far away from God. It is one of the reasons that we meet resistance even in churches. It has even led to splitting of churches.

God continued to visit Joseph in dreams and this time it was the sun and the moon and the eleven stars that made obeisance to him. This time around, God was more specific and the interpretation of this dream was not difficult for the father.

"Shall I and thy mother and thy brethren indeed come to bow down ourselves to thee to the earth?"

It was a serious dream and instead of his brothers teaming up with him to bring about the realization of this dream, envy was the response. They failed to realize that in most generations there is usually a figure-head that God elects and uses. Their plan instead was to ensure that his dreams were not realized. Many of us are fund of quickly revealing our visions and dreams to other people. Most of the time, they will quietly plan that those dreams and visions God has shown to us do not come to pass. It is usually the plan of the devil. Even for Jesus, he planned that He should be killed by causing Herod to decree that all children that were 2 years old and under (Matt. 1:16) should be killed. I am sure it was clear to Joseph that his brothers did not like him, yet when his father told him to go and see if all was well with them, he did not hesitate. Even when he did not find them easily he pressed on until he saw them in Dothan (Genesis 37:17). At this point his brothers decided to kill him. I am sure he was seriously disappointed with his brothers. Although all the brothers had conspired to kill him, God was quietly making arrangement to save him. Ishmaelite business men came at that point and were willing to purchase him for 20 pieces of silver. That was how God spared his life. I am sure that Joseph saw himself at this point as a disappointment. How will all the dreams come to pass now that he is separated from his parents? After all they were the ones doing obeisance in the dream that he dreamt. God, however, had a plan. God does not use a man that he does not "make." It is usually **"follow me and I will make you......"** If only we can lean to follow God without complaining. I thank God for men like Joseph. In all his trouble he continued to follow God, even as a slave as we shall soon see.

One thing we must carefully note is that God does not use us in the comfort of our homes. It is usually **"I have chosen thee in the furnace of affliction"** (Isaiah 48:10). Joseph could not be used of God in the comfort of his father's home. He had to be separated to a place where no one knows him. At such a place he will be forced to look up only onto God. No father, no step-mother, no half-brother, no brother.

In fact, there was no one to comfort him. That is the desert of life where God actually trains his people and ordains them into their destiny as he did into Moses. I am sure Joseph and Benjamin being the children from the beloved wife of Jacob, Rachael, would usually eat with their father with extra meat and other entrails. The coat of many colours was gone. There was no Benjamin to call at play time.

He began to live and eat the food meant for slaves. He could be killed anytime just because of one careless mistake or just because they want to use him for entertainment or one ceremony. All that will see him through now is uprightness. He must walk closely with God. Any careless life-style will end his life and his destiny. We are told that his original buyers resold him to Potiphar. He became a commodity. In all these, the Bible recorded clearly that the Lord was with him (Genesis 39:2). Then came the temptation from Potiphar's wife, asking Joseph to sleep with her. To us that would have been harmless as Joseph would have been getting more favour. His meal would have been assured even before that of his master. He would have had permanent and secret "appointment" with the woman. That would mean losing appointment with God. He had to risk his life. Many of us cannot change our generation because of wanting too much favour from men. It becomes something important if the president or the congress of our country should call us to speak to them. Some people think that the more the people they know the better for them. Actually no one knows you unless God has known you. The number of people that knows you is proportional to the level that God knows you. Even while Joseph was in prison, if God had not known him, He would not have caused Pharaoh to have a dream. The man who knew him forgot to say anything about him once he was out of prison (Genesis 40: 23). Even men that want to favour you, God has to remind them. Thus, Joseph was severally disappointed by people. Men will disappoint you. If you do not know God, such disappointment could even end your life.

CHAPTER 9
NAOMI AND RUTH

The stories of the two women, Naomi and Ruth are two good examples of disappointments women easily face in life. In many societies there are large numbers of widows just as the case of these too women. The stories of these two women cannot, however, be told separately, as there can be no Ruth without a Naomi.

Naomi was an Israelite and Ruth was not. Their story, therefore, clearly exemplified how God can bring disappointment into the life of any man or woman from any tribe or race. Naomi followed her husband Elimelech to the land of Moab in search of food. Many great men of God in the Bible went down to cities that may be termed ungodly in search of food. It may be a sign that God, in His infinite mercy can show them favour and visit them. Abraham went down to Egypt in search of food. Jacob and his descendants went to Egypt in search of food. These were places that one can refer to as heathen nations. Egypt was symbolic of a heathen nation in the Old Testament. Moabite was typical of a polluted nation – a nation with polluted foundation. The nation of Moab came into existence as a result of the incest relationship between Lot and his first daughter (Genesis 19:30-38). God had said of the Moabites that they shall not enter unto the congregation of the Lord. Incest is a serious sin and God does not tolerate such behaviour. In our degenerate society, people no longer take such sins serious. All people involved in such sins should cry out to God for help. His mercies endure for ever. When the children of Israel where conquering nations to possess the Land, God insisted that the tribe of Moab should be spared

(Deuteronomy 2:9). When God's appointed time came, he allowed Elimelech and her family to go and dwell in the land of Moab. In the eyes of men, it is hunger that sent this family there. Similarly, in the eyes of men it is hunger that made Abraham to go down to Egypt. The Bible says that all things work for good to them that love God (Romans 6:28). When Abraham went in search of food to Egypt, he caused God to visit them. At least the hand of God was heavy upon the king of Egypt. When God visits a king, there must be influence upon his people as he will keep telling them how powerful the God of Abraham was. Pharaoh had to warn all his people concerning Abraham and his wife (Genesis 12: 12-20). That is enough preaching.

Do not however, see this as an opportunity to do illegal migration. Abraham did not come out free. His journey into Egypt made him to tell lies that Sarah was not his wife! He also came out of Egypt with Hagar that became trouble in the family and for generations to come. The most ardent enemies of Christians today are the children of this bond woman. Jacob also went to Egypt. Unfortunately for him, he did not live to return. He died there. His death was, however, was not in vain. When his descendants were leaving there many years later some of the Egyptians had repented and followed. The Bible recorded that a mixed multitude left Egypt (Exodus 12:40-41).

Like Elimelech and his family, Abraham and Sarah, Jacob and his family, many Nigerians and people from other Third World Countries have moved in "search of food" to other nations of the world. These, like the group of people mentioned above have gone to their own "Egypt" and what may become of them may also be like what happened to this people. Some may die there. Some may lose their family members. These days it is easy to lose one's family members to the devil, even if they are not physically dead, in some advance countries where the devil is on the rampage, in form of hard drugs, pornography and other vices. Some may return with a "Hagar." In all these, what is important is whether we will still be with God. The stories of the people are in the Bible today because of their walk with God. It will be a pity for any man to lose out completely because he has gone in search of "food" to a "far country" like the prodigal son. Remember too that the prodigal son returned to his father.

Back to the story of Ruth and Naomi. Naomi lost her husband and her two sons. I am sure there is no disappointment greater than this in life. Ruth too must have been extremely disappointed after losing her husband at such an early age. Apart from the pains of widowhood, her mother-in-law was from a strange country. At last Naomi had to return to her own country and to her people. Ruth decided to follow her after much insistence. Orpah decided to stay back in Moab. She was not sure of what would become of her. Ruth followed her mother in-law into the unknown. In fact, on their return to the land of Israel what to eat was even a problem.

At the instruction of her mother-in-law she had to go and glean in the farm of a man she did know (Ruth 2). Again at the instance of Naomi, her mother-in-law, she had to go and almost plead to be married by Boaz her father's -in-law relative. Her life was marked by great strides of faith and obedience. A combination of these two virtues will also lead any person to have a good standing with God. No wonder, this Moabite woman was able to have a place in the genealogy of Jesus Christ the Saviour (Mathew 1:5).

CHAPTER 10

DISAPPOINTMENTS OF THE PROPHETS

The prophets of God were another disappointed group. Many were disappointed both with God and with men. Their major disappointment with God was because they knew that the power of God was awesome and as such He should protect them from all dangers. God never did that. On the other hand, they knew what could become of the earth if only they could convince men to follow God. All their cries were never hidden to.

One thing about disappointment is that there must be "something" one has seen and yet unable to accomplish it. The prophets saw the awesome power of God. They saw what beauty could become of the earth. They saw what peace will accrue to the earth if only men followed God.

These were never to be, and has never been. Even God threatening curses upon the earth as shown Deuteronomy 12 and 28 never changed the behavior of men. There were pockets of men in what may be called a revival that may seem to completely follow God in every generation, yet there were deviants among them. Sometimes it was just a man or two among the entire nation that were revived. This is the same in all generations. Why it is in the nature of man of man to desire to disobey God, may be difficult to know, but I simply want to say that it is the nature of evil acquired during the fall of Adam. This nature is always rebellious against God since He is the overall definition of anything good. All that God wants us to be does not better His life or enhance His being God. It is all for the benefit of man, yet man behaves as if it will add something to God. We try to make God a politician so that we can vote for Him. This is horrible.

Moses could "see' the Promised Land afar off. He could see the beauty of the land with its condiments. He could see the peace and authority the Israelites would enjoy if they settled down in the Promised Land. The Israelites saw differently. They knew only the acts of God while Moses knew the way of God (Acts 103:7). Since they did not have the same vision with Moses it was almost practically impossible for him to lead them to the Promised Land. All they were interested with was what God could give them now and not any future. They needed good food, enjoyment, e.t.c. and as such always remembered the cucumbers of Egypt! They were ready to be slaves if only that could be the source of their food. They could only remember what they ate. Many of us today are like them. We prefer to be in bondage instead of being under God and have freedom. In some part of third world country beggars in the street usually inflict some form of disease upon themselves so as to be able to use that as a reason for begging. You know in the Bible, Jesus would often ask such beggars if they wanted to receive healing so as not to remove their source of livelihood. You also know the story about Paul and Silas in the Bible. They healed a lady possessed with the spirit of divination or future (fortune-)-telling (Acts 16:16-24). It became their source of persecution and imprisonment. The lady who was healed used her sickness (her demon possession) as a source of income for her masters. The Book of Deuteronomy was a kind of a reminder and a plea (the valedictory lecture of Moses) to Israelites so that they should not return to Egypt. I am sure at this point Moses was utterly disappointed with the Israelites.

Under Moses they knew nothing about sickness and diseases because the Bible recorded that none among them was feeble. Their clothes and sandals did not wear out.

Was Deuteronomy just a valedictory lecture? I think it was a valedictory lecture from a disappointed man to an "impossible generation" much less difficult than our own. If Phinehas, the son of Aaron, were alive now, I wonder how many people he will thrust through with his javelin (numbers 25: 6-8). A generation that does not decipher sin from holiness can make any man to be disappointed. Today many blame the pastors of the church. Some accuse them of obeying the slogan, "if you cannot beat them, join them." Actually many pastors have been caught in the web of sin because we live in a generation where sin is celebrated. I think the anointing that one needs now to live a sin-free life must be something more that what our fathers-in-the-faith had. In his own valedictory speech, Joshua could only tell the people of Israel, **"Choose this day whom you will serve; whether the gods which your fathers served that were on the other side of the flood or the goods of the Amorites, in whose land you dwell; but us for me and mine house we will serve the Lord."** I also see this as a sentence of frustration from Joshua. I thank God that in his time, there was a "flood" that separated them from the gods that they served beyond the river. In our generation, there is no flood that can separate us from sin. Sin seems to be knocking on every door, with pornographic pictures, nude women, e.t.c. at every corner of the street. Joshua and the Israelites had a choice. No wonder, Jesus said, the time for his return has to be shortened for the sake of the elect.

Back to the issue of disappointments of the prophets; one man that was thoroughly disappointed was Samuel. Samuel was loved by Samuel particularly as he was chosen by God after the Israelites demanded for a king. Yet Saul misbehaved. One of the greatest things the world is suffering from today is bad leadership. The societies that are suffering from hunger, disease, war, e.t.c., are largely due to bad leadership. Saul, the son of Kish was a man that Samuel loved particularly as he was the one that anointed him as king of Israel. He was like his spiritual son. Moreover, not only did he anoint him as king, he was available to advise him and lead him in a godly path. Yet Saul fell to the utter disappointment of Samuel. One painful thing about the fall of Saul was that he was occupying a position that he did not even qualify for. He was a Benjamite. I am sure he never prayed or nursed the ambition for any office like that. Only the tribe of Judah actually has the privilege of producing Israeli kings. In fact, Israel had not even had a king before him. These are enough reasons for Samuel to pray and weep for Saul. It was God, Himself, who spoke to Samuel saying, ***"How long will you mourn for Saul, seeing I have rejected him from reigning over Israel? Fill thine horn with oil and go, I will send you to Jesse the Bethlehemite. For I have provided for myself a king among his sons."*** I am sure God did this to tell Samuel that He was not going back on the issue of Saul. He was rejected and remained rejected. You can imagine that not only Samuel was disappointed with Saul, but God was also disappointed with him.

One other disappointment I want to quickly state about the story of Samuel in the Bible was that, God did not tell him to anoint one of his sons. God was looking for a godly man, yet that could not be found in the house of the spiritual leader of Israel to replace Saul. In fact, what even brought Saul to the throne was that the Israelites sought for a godly king in Samuel's house but could find none (1 Samuel 8:1-5). For men who concentrate on the work of God at the expense of one's family, this should ring a bell. After the era of Samuel, many people who came to the throne of Israel were very ungodly. A godly family should try as much as possible to produce seed that could replace them.

Was the issue of disappointments better with the later prophets? The answer is simply No! Isaiah, Jeremiah, Ezekiel, e.t.c., had their own share. The burden of disappointment was so much upon Jeremiah that he had to write his book of Lamentations. Isaiah must have seen himself as a failure when God had to advertise his job. **"Whom shall I send? And who will go for us?"** (Isaiah 6:8). This shows that God was dissatisfied with him. Isaiah must also have been disappointed when he heard that he was not performing satisfactorily on his job. Many of us are like him-filled with many activities for God yet not according to set pattern. Isaiah was not idle. He was a prophet in Uzziah's house until he died.

Until the "Uzziahs" in our life also die, we may never be free to do the Master's will. Remember that after the death of Uzziah, Isaiah became a fiery preacher to a troublesome nation. He could remind them thus: ***"Hear you oh house of David; is it a small thing for you to weary men; but will you weary my God also?"*** This is a sign of complete disappointment. It seems that he knew that God was even getting tired with the nation of Israel. The story was not different for Jeremiah. Men have given him the name of the weeping prophet! Who will not weep when a nation turns its back on God? Who will not weep when he realizes the danger that faces the un-regenerated here and the hereafter? When one sees the wars, natural disasters and other calamities that are befalling our generation, all because we have turned our backs on God, who will not weep? When we hear of earthquakes that kill thousands, who will not weep? When we hear of the AIDS pandemic that has depopulated some parts of the world, who will not weep? Jeremiah was weeping for the Israelites because he saw afar off what their leaders could not see. If there is any genuine prophet of God, today, he should be weeping all day long! Three-year olds are being raped and murdered. There are street killers in every corner. Assassins have multiplied even in regions of the world once thought to be peaceful. The entire earth is simply currently a war zone. We hear of nuclear pile-ups here and there. There is the issue of global warning ascribed largely to green houses that unfriendly to the ozone layer. I also ascribe it also to the age of the earth. The earth is aging! Creation is groaning (Romans 8: 21, 22). Yes every aspect of creation is expected to be subjected to corruption until it is delivered (Romans 8:21). And no deliverance will come until the sons of God are delivered. With the increase in sin on the surface of the earth, deliverance is pushed further away. We should therefore, not only weep but also groan.

In fact our generation is similar to that of Elijah. After a hot battle with the prophets of Baal, he had to declare that he was the only prophet in the land. It took the Almighty God Himself to let him know that there were 7000 prophets who had not bowed their knees to Baal (1 Kings 19). I therefore say with trembling that genuine Christianity is almost extinct from our land. There is now no difference between the sacred and the profane. There is no difference in the character and manner of Christians and the world. Let us raise our voices to God and cry for mercy for our generation.

CHAPTER 11
THE DISAPPOINTMENT OF JESUS

I have treated the disappointment of God but will also have to treat Jesus differently. He was God, yet he is the pattern for everything. No Christian write-up is worth its salt without tying it up on Jesus. First of all, He is the pattern for everything including disappointment. The father Himself made it clear that we should listen to him.

I am sure this was the reason for the transfiguration. The law and the prophets (typified by Moses and Elijah) are all inferior to Him. Whatever the law and the prophets said are inferior to what Jesus says. It was for this purpose that the Father has to declare during the transfiguration, **"This is my beloved Son, in whom I am well pleased, hear ye Him"** (Matt. 17: 1- 9). Yes, whatever Jesus says about disappointments is correct. Whatever happened around Him when he was working in the streets of Jerusalem has much to be learnt from.

Jesus was a symbol of disappointment from birth to death. Such a being that came from Heaven was expected to be born in a wealth family, with all the celebrations and naming ceremonies. These were not to be. He was born quietly in a manger where only His father and mother and sheep were his companions. Human beings are never comfortable with such a happening. If being born quietly was what heaven wanted why not at least in a popular town? After all, no prophet has ever comes from Galilee!

This has much lesson for us. Many of the things that have heavenly origin happen quietly without much fanfare! That is why many people are left behind even when God has moved into doing a new thing. For human beings whatever

God does must be loud and clear. This is usually not the case. This was the lesson Elijah had to learn on Mount Horeb (1 Kings 19:11-14). Elijah had thought that the visitation of God had to be accompanied with boisterous wind, thunder and/or earthquake, but this was not to be. God came at a time when everything was still. This is the nature of our God.

The other thing that must have brought about some disappointments in the life of Jesus was that the parents were not to name the child. The child's name was given from above. The parents had nothing to contribute. Moreover, the name given was not even the type that was common in Israel. None of their relatives bore that name. It is usually important that male children pick names of their family members for the continuation or perpetuation of the generational lineage. Other parents would want to give names to their parents that would bring prosperity into the life of the children. Thus names such as "Goodluck", "Godswill", Godspower, e.t.c. are common these days. For Jesus, this was not to be so.

Another disappointment during the early life of Jesus was that his birth brought death to many children. This must have brought sorrow to very many families. I keep wondering what the parents of the children that were two years and under that were slaughtered will be saying when they found that Jesus was not killed along with their own children. That will forever create enmity between Him and these parents. After all it was because of Him that their own children were killed. If Jesus was killed too, the story might be different.

At other times too Jesus was a disappointment to his father and mother. We are told how the family used to visit Jerusalem yearly at the feast of the Passover (Luke 2: 42-50).

One of the years that they went with Jesus, he could not be found when the parents had travelled a day's journey.

He had disappointed them as they had to go back in search of Him. They assumed He was with their relatives. It is good for us not to assume like these parents (Joseph and Mary) that Jesus was coming along with us of with our relatives. He must personally be with us for the journey of life to be smooth. Many of us believe that Jesus is with one man of God or the other. Sometimes we believe He is in our church without checking out our personal life. In fact it is a risk to think like this. Supposing we do not have him? It will be too unfortunate because there is no possibility of eternal life without Him. Jesus in you is the hope of glory (Col. 1:27, 28). We must therefore, never leave him behind in the church before we encounter a terrible disappointment.

His three years ministry upon the surface of the earth was filled with disappointment. It came to a point that his follower had to leave him, with only the 12 disciples remaining with him (John 6). He was a disappointment to both his disciples and his parents. His disciples left different trades to follow him. Leaving them at this point meant much to them. Many would be left stranded. At this age of maturity (30 years and above) is the period that most people take care of their parents yet he had to die leaving this duty back-stage.

Jesus was also disappointed by His disciples. After His resurrection he had told his disciples to wait till they were empowered from up high. Two of his disciples decided to travel to Emmaus. Peter and some of them went fishing (John 20:.....). Similarly, He commissioned His disciples to start preaching from Jerusalem to Judea and the uttermost parts of the world. They never did until persecution started.

Michael Adikwu

CHAPTER 12
THE GAINS OF DISAPPOINTMENT

The above chapters have only pointed out the pains of disappointment. I want to say very quickly that disappointment is training. It is the way God trains his people. As earlier mentioned no man can enter his rest until God has passed through some level of training. This training is usually not palatable. The bible likens the relationship between God and his children to that of the pot and the potter. We are the pot, God is the potter. **Knowing God's pattern for training is a very crucial matter for us to be able to allow Him to mold us to the shape He wants; not we want.** Everyman that God uses must be refined in the furnace of affliction (Isaiah 48:10).

Disappointment builds up. A man who is disappointed with men automatically takes appointment with God if he manages the disappointment well. When God became disappointed with men he had appointment with them through his son Jesus Christ. This "appointment" of god with men is the mother of all "appointments". It brought with it all that can be thought. It brought to an end, the activity of God's and man's enemy the Devil. All the pains that accrue to men actually come from this "appointment" with the devil. It is the origin of death which is the greatest disappointment that has bedeviled human existence on earth. It brought with it sickness. It brought with it jealously, murder, wickedness and the evil any man can think of in this life.

The exact opposite of appointment of men with the devil is what happens when a man has appointment with God. All that have power over him in a negative direction is tuned towards the position side.

An "Appointment" with God also overthrows the self. There are others who may have vowed never to have an appointment with the devil but they quietly have appointment with themselves. A man that has appointment with himself, cannot have appointment with God. Are you surprised that in these days we hear of self-reliance, self confident, self-dependence, self this, self that. All these are to break any reliance on God. A man who walks by depending on himself is at the same footing with the devil in relationship to God. This is because the Bible says that those that walk according to the dictates of the flesh are in enmity with God. (Romans 8:7). A man that has "lost" appointment with self also begins to enjoy appointment with God. Temptations lose their power in the life of such a man. He has no room for pride which is the major factor that self walks with. Self becomes powerful when it want to make a name for itself. In such a situation God is left-backstage and may be called upon to come and make a name for self or even add value to this. As far as God is not willing to do this, self may look for other means of achieving this. It may be through outright substitution of one false god for the genuine Almighty God. Such gods may even come in from of politics. It may be money or wine. It may be women. It may be fame. It may be a secret cult. It may be one traditional god or the other. All these lose their power in the life of many men once we have appointment with God. It therefore, seems right to say that one must be disappointed by all these gods to have a genuine appointment with God.

CHAPTER 13
DISAPPOINTMENT AND THE DESERT LIFE

Disappointments take men to their deserts. In the church, in the market, at home, I see the restleness that befalls man. Man is ever restless thinking, planning and struggling to achieve one thing or the other. When a man becomes disappointment with life, he looks for a lonely place where he is often alone with God. Moses became disappointed with life in Egypt, and among his brethren the Israelites and escaped to Midian. It was while here that he could encounter God in the desert. Suppose he was not disappointed in his people and remained with them. He could even become a king but his story would have been different from what we know today. What about Abraham? I am sure he was a disappointment to his nuclear family. At the age when he left Haran, his age mates may be preparing for their own burial. Yet he embarked on a journey into the desert of life. In Canaan, he had no relatives who would be calling one family meeting or the other. He had no extended family. He could commune with God. Back home in Haran, there were family disputes to settle. Being the eldest man he might even have sacrifices to offer for other members of the extended family. Any time any one dies, he has to be there for the burial. If there were ceremonies such as marriage or naming ceremonies, Abraham must be present. Away from home, in Canaan, all these were no longer a matter to Abraham. As such he could seek and develop a strong tie with God. Do you wonder then that men like Abraham had such a strong tie with God? No wonder that Jesus had to say to the multitude.

"If any man comes to me and does not hate his father and mother, his wife and children, his brothers and sisters - yes, even his own life – he cannot be my disciple."

These classes of people (father, mother, wife, children, brothers and sisters) are obstacles to our walk with God. One of the gains of these people being disappointed with as or we being disappointed with them is a closer walk with God with its attendant benefits.

Can you imagine what would have become of Joseph if he was not separated from his family ties? Joseph was left in the midst of hostile brothers after the death of his mother. His mother was a nagging woman if one careful studies the life of Jacobs's family, I keep wondering what would have become of the life of Joseph! At best, a violent young man with history like those, have ended like that of his brother, Benjamin. He is not given any special mention among the twelve tribes of Israel. We read of how Joseph became governor in Egypt because disappointment took him to where he could be alone with God. Disappointment took him to a place where he could realize his destiny. In prison, in Egypt, he could commune with God on a one to one basis. He had only God as his true companion.

If there is so much gain in disappointment, do we wander, then why early Church Fathers practiced the life of separation? Many of them became monks. It was during their ascetic life that many of them genuinely encountered God. They understood what we do not seem to understand today. The hustle of everyday life has a way of interfering in our walk with God. It is only a few disciplined men and women that can genuinely encountered God. They understood what we do not seem to understand today. The hustle and bustle of everyday life has a way of interfering in our walk with God. It is only a few disciplined men and women that can genuinely practice the presence of God in Everyday life. In everyday life there is the problem of the cravings of the flesh – what to eat and drink. These battles are often reduced when men are disappointed with life. Men who genuinely want to seek the face of God must also reduce these craving be it in the matter of food, drink, or women.

CHAPTER 14
DISAPPOINTMENT AND PRAYER LIFE

Godly men pray when there is a disappointment. Even for Jesus his prayer life was influenced by the disappointments he received from his people, the Israelites and particularly from the religions leaders of his time. The scripture records that,

"During the Days of Jesus' Life on earth, he offered up prayers and petitions with loud cries and tears to the One who could save him from death, and he was heard because of his present submission. Although he was a son, he learned obedience from what he suffered and, once made perfect, he became the source of eternal salvation for all who obey him and was designated by God to be high priest in order of Melchizedek".

Disappointment brought Jesus to the point of raising daily prayers to His Father with loud cries and tears (Hebrew 5:7). The Bible said that He was perfected through what he suffered. The greatest level of suffering came from the disappointment of Jesus with his own people. Through this disappointment he was killed. If his people were satisfied with him, he would not have been killed.

In fact at the point of death, Jesus was disappointed in God. The cry of Jesus, My God, my God, why have you forsaken me" was a cry of disappointment. All in all, through these series of disappointments and resultant prayers and the death of our LORD Jesus Christ the whole world is gained for God.

What about the early prophets. Jeremiah was simply called the weeping prophet. His tears were tears of prayers. Disappointment brings burdens to one's soul. For a man to pray with tears shows the burden he is bearing within.

What about Daniel? Daniel was so disappointed with the state of affairs with his people the Israelites that he prayed three times daily (Daniel 6:13).

Every disappointment Daniel had with the people of the land of his captivity drove him to pray more. The same situation was around the life of Esther. In the land of their captivity, the Israelites were facing extermination in the hand of Human the Agagite. There are always Hamans around to bring disappointments and discomfort to the children of God. For Esther, and her people, the situation drove them to prayers and fasting. The situation was not different for Nehemiah.

Nehemiah was so disappointed with the situation of the Israelites and the state of the wall of Jerusalem as well as the temple that he decided to weep. He was not just weeping but weeping in prayers. The resultant effect was that he was allowed to go and build the walls of Jerusalem. Many "broken walls" in our lives will only be amended when we reach this level of sorrow. This can be brought about by disappointment when we become dissatisfied with the situations around us. When Jeremiah became disappointed with his people he became a "weeping prophet." He was weeping for the terrible things that would befall the children of Israel.

CHAPTER 15
GAINS OF DISAPPOINTMENTS THAT LED TO DEATH

The Bible was quick to mention that the early saints overcome the enemy by the Blood of the Lamb and that they died even as witnesses with their lives.

And they overcame him by the blood of the Lamb, and by the word of their testimony; and they loved not their lives unto death (Revelation 12:11).

Let us here take a look at the history of the lives, sufferings and deaths of some of the early Christian martyrs. The information presented herewith is derived from two basic sources: *Fox's Book of Martyrs* and *Fox's Christian Martyrs of the World* as obtained from the Internet. Both of these books are must reads for any serious scholar of Christianity. And certainly should be read by those interested in the vast persecution that pervaded the early Church and its founding disciples and apostles.

Jesus Christ

The very first martyr in the name of God is of course, Jesus Christ of Nazareth. Of that there is no question. His death on the cross for all mankind, for all generations is the first, indeed most important, case of martyrdom for Christianity. All the gains we have had in the Faith today emanated from him. There is no religion that has not gained from the death and resurrection of Jesus Christ. It may be in physical matters of holiday or even the Sabbath Day. There is nowhere in the world where Saturday and Sunday are not recognised as days of rest with the resultant gains of vitality and the attendant health improvement. Paul consistently presented Jesus as the archetypal martyr and as an example for all Christians; therefore, it is not surprising that early Church documents on martyrdom considered Jesus to be the prototype of the martyr. The Bible has a great deal to say about persecution and the battle waged between the Kingdom of God and the forces of this world as influenced by Satan.

Without the offence of the cross, there would be no mission, but also no persecution (Galatians 5:11). Paul accused his opponents of being circumcised only to escape persecution (Galatians 6:12, 14). Indeed, the word of the cross is foolishness to unbelievers (1 Corinthians 1:18), an impediment to the Jews, and nonsense to the Gentiles (1 Corinthians 1:23); however, it is also the centre of salvation history (1 Corinthians 1:23; 2:2). The message of the cross is thus the glory of the gospel, as well as its foolishness (1 Corinthians 1:17-25; Galatians 6:11-14)

\

Stephen

The next martyr was Stephen. His death was a direct result of his preaching the Gospel and the faithful manner in which he exclaimed the glory of the Lord, even unto those betrayers and murders of Christ. Stephen was stoned to death in the street at Passover the Spring following Jesus' Crucifixion. The outrage Stephen caused was so great that there was great persecution of the Church through the regions of Judea and Samaria, particularly in Jerusalem. It is said that over 2,000 Christians suffered persecution and death as a direct result of Stephen.)

James

The next martyr was James, the son of Zebedee, elder brother of John. James' martyrdom was about 10 years after the death of Stephen. This occurred under the hand of the infamous Herod Agrippa who was determined not only to persecute the Christians but indeed annihilate them. James was undaunted when confronted with his impending death; when he was brought to the place of martyrdom, he continued to preach and exhort those around. His main accuser was so moved by the Apostle's conviction; this man repented and fell down at

James' feet! Then, both men were beheaded at the same time!

Philip

Born at Bethsaida, in Galilee, he was one of the first to be called 'disciple'. He labored for Christ throughout Upper Asia and suffered martyrdom at Heliopolis, in Phrygia. He was scourged, thrown into prison and then crucified.

Matthew

Matthew was the tax collector that left all when Jesus simply said 'Follow me.' He was born at Nazareth. He wrote his entire gospel in Hebrew, but thanks to James, the Gospel of Matthew was translated into Greek. Matthew laboured for our Lord in Parthia, and Ethiopia where he suffered his death being slain by chopping apart by halberd.

James

He was the head of all the Churches of Jerusalem and the author of the Epistle in the New Testament bearing his name. At the age of 94, he was beaten and stoned by the Jews, still not dying they bashed his brains out with a club.

Matthias

Less is known about him than most of the other disciples, but he was elected to fill the place of Judas. He was stoned at Jerusalem and then beheaded.

Andrew

He was the brother of Peter. He preached the gospel to many Asiatic nations; but when he arrived at Odessa, he was seized and crucified on a cross, the two ends of which were fixed transversely in the ground; hence the derivation of the term, St. Andrew's Cross.

Mark

Mark was a Jew, born of the tribe of Levi. Very important tribe in the Jewish nation. He was converted to Christianity by Peter. In conjunction with Peter, he wrote the Gospel of Mark in the Greek language (instead of Hebrew which was his natural tongue). Mark was literally dragged and torn to pieces by the people of Alexandria.

Peter

The blessed Apostle Peter, the one whom Jesus declared to build his Church upon, was condemned to death at Rome by Nero. However, Peter had several, indeed many opportunities to escape. Many offered Peter refuge. He refused all. Peter recounts that while he was at the Gate of the city, preparing to flee, he saw Jesus Christ come down to meet him; worshipping Christ, Peter said that the Lord indicated that he was come again to be crucified. By this, Peter perceived that he was to be crucified for the Lord, and returned to the city. He ask that he be crucified with his head down and his feet upward, he being unworthy to be crucified in the same form and manner as the Lord.

Paul

Paul also suffered persecution and ultimately death under the hand of Nero. Two messengers of Nero, Ferega and Parthemius, were dispatched to Paul to tell him of his impending death. When they got to Paul, he was preaching the Word of God and instructing people in the way of the Lord; these messengers indicated that they too wanted to believe and wanted Paul to lead them in prayer. As Paul bowed in prayer, they beheaded him.

Jude

The brother of James was commonly called Thaddeus. He was crucified at Odessa.

Bartholomew

He preached in many countries, often translating the Gospel into the native language, including India where he was cruelly beaten and crucified.

Thomas

Also called Didymus, preached the Gospel in Parthia and India, where the pagan priests killed him by thrusting a spear through him.

Luke

The evangelist and author of the Gospel that carries his name. He traveled with Paul through various countries. He was hanged to death from an olive tree in Greece.

Simon

Preached the Gospel in Africa and even Great Britain, where he was crucified.

John

The 'beloved disciple' was a brother to James. He founded many Churches, including Smyrna, Pergamos, Sardis, Philadelphia, Laodicea, and Thyatira. Captured at Ephesus, he was taken to Rome where he was put into a cauldron of hot, boiling oil. By a miracle of God, he was taken out without any injury! Domitian immediately banished him to the Isle of Patmos, where John wrote the book of Revelation. He is the only disciple of Christ to escape violent death.

The lives of the martyrs became a great source of inspiration for the early Christians and their lives were greatly revered. Second century Church Father, Tertullian wrote that "The blood of martyrs is the seed of the Church", implying that the willing sacrificing of the martyrs' lives leads to the conversion of many more. The age of martyrdom also helped develop some of the worship patterns.

Christ-followers are persecuted all over the world simply for what they believe. According to the United States State Department, Christians in over 60 countries face the realities of massacre, rape, torture, mutilation, family division, harassment, imprisonment, slavery, discrimination in education and employment, and even death.

As Paul Marshall describes persecution in his book "Their Blood Cries Out" persecution of Christians is real but the gains are enormous. The Bible says that all followers of Jesus Christ should expect persecution (2 Timothy 3:12) and suggests that persecution leads to church growth. God can work out good in any and all circumstances.

It has been said that "persecution is a storm that is permitted to scatter the seed of the Word, and disperse the sower and reaper over many fields. It is God's way of extending his kingdom."

So persecution often accompanies missions, for "missions lead to martyrdom, and martyrdom becomes missions." Jesus warned his disciples that they were going out as sheep in the midst of wolves (Matthew 10:16; Luke 10:3). The universal spread of Christ's Church has always been accompanied with the blood of the martyrs; world mission is "mission beneath the cross." Church history contains many descriptions of dying Christians, such as Polycarp, who prayed for those tormenting them.

The modern Church has its own examples. In 1913, the Indonesian evangelist, Petrus Octavianus, described a missionary in the Toradya area in southern Celebes. Five tribe members wanted to kill the missionary, but permitted him to pray first. He prayed aloud that they would be saved. Three of the murderers were banned to Java, were converted in prison, and returned to Toradya, where they founded a church which later (1971) became the fourth largest church in Indonesia. Let us also not forget the five missionaries shot to death by the Aucas in Equador in the 1960s. Several of the murderers later became pillars of the Aucan church.

Many who began as persecutors of Christians later became believers themselves. The best known is Paul, who frequently referred to his former persecution of the Church (1 Corinthians 15:9; Galatians 1:13, 23-24; Philippians 3:6; 1 Timothy 1:13; Acts 9:4-5, 22: 4, 7-8; 16:11, 14-15).

Can anyone explain how the churches in the countries where persecution is most prominent are the ones growing most rapidly? They are growing not only in maturity but in numbers. Remember, they cannot afford to openly invite their neighbours to Christian meetings. Evangelism takes place in the lives of those believers even through their sufferings. In their meetings they worship God and pray for His will, and ask for strength so that they will stand strong and not deny their Lord and Saviour in times of trouble. They support each other spiritually and even with their possessions. They even pray for those in other lands where there is no persecution. They pray that Christians in such places will wake up and be alert and follow Christ so that they will not be caught unawares.

Many times a cell church will only have one Bible or only a portion of a Bible. Just being caught with it could cost them many years in prison or even death. Yet it is the most precious of all books to them. They pass it around and each person memorizes as much as he can so that he can hide it in his heart. Not out of obligation, or some abstract idea that a good Christian should memorize Scripture, but because it is life to them, it is God's word and it is their strength. What other gain can be greater than this-that a man is always prepared should death come unannounced?

Chapter 16
Why do Men Hate Disappointment?

Disappointment has element of trouble and suffering. These two words, trouble and suffering, are dreaded by men on the surface of the earth.

The world is generally full of troubles but the ability to calm these troubles is by the Spirit of the living God. I do not want to start by defining what troubles are; anything that causes discomfort is a trouble including diseases. Anything that makes one uneasy is trouble. I do not wonder about this because in the beginning when God created the world it was so. It may be called by different names. Some call it persecution; others call it tribulation, etc. In the beginning when God created the world it was engulfed in darkness. Some Bible versions say the world was without form. Others say it was chaotic. These are all forms of trouble. When a man is in trouble he is engulfed in darkness. His life is formless. He can be looking at a person and will not even see the person physically because of the darkness.

Everything around such person is chaotic. Life around him has no shape. Even in the story of creation that also took place. What brings order to every situation is the Spirit of God. When the Spirit of God hovered around the chaotic earth, order came in (Genesis 1: 1-3).

We are in the World

Jesus made it clear that we are in the world but not of the world (John 15:19). God was aware that the world will always be chaotic so He made man to put order in the world. Man is the most organised of all God's creation. In fact, where there is disorganisation, God expects man to bring in organisation. He made man in His image (carrying the Spirit of God) to keep this order. All creation groans waiting for the manifestation of the sons of God (Romans 8: 19-22). Anyone that loses sight of this will be creating a chaotic atmosphere around himself. One thing with the word of God is that it does not change. The Bible says that the entire world lies in darkness, in the grip of the evil one (1 John 5: 19). As Christians, we must work in the consciousness of this to be able to survive. A man walking (and even working) in the dark must be careful if not he will hit an obstacle. In fact, even cars slow down at night. One good thing is that light dispels darkness. The ability to bear this light in the midst of competing options is the challenge of Christians. The Bible enjoins us to present our bodies as a living sacrifice, holy, acceptable unto God (Romans 12: 1-2). In fact, the Bible went on to say that this is our "reasonable" sacrifice. Can I inform you that other things you are sacrificing your life for are not reasonable. In fact, all earthly things you are sacrificing your life for other than God are not reasonable.

Trouble is Meant to Build You

When a man is carrying the light of God, troubles are meant to build him and not to mar him. It must be pointed out, however, that the way you handle your trouble will determine whether it will enlarge or destroy you. People who manage the trouble well emerge stronger than before the trouble came. Others who mismanage their troubles get frustrated or even destroyed. For instance, Hanna in the Bible managed her trouble well (1 Samuel 1).

One chaotic environment that often brings much stress to a family is polygamous marriage. Hannah found herself in one with her husband Elkanah. Nature had made her barren. Apart from the trouble of bareness, she had an adversary as the second wife of her husband whose name was Peninnah. For the Bible to have called her an "adversary" means she really troubled Hannah. She was a real problem for her to handle. Instead of handling it the way of the world through quarrelling and fighting, she took the battle to the Lord through prayers. That broke the double-barrelled chain of barrenness and trouble from Peninnah. She gave birth to a man who became the president of Israel. In fact, none of the children of the second wife, Peninnah, was worthy of mention in the Bible. Hannah's son became a role model in terms of governance, priesthood and even prophecy over Israel. All women, barren or not, should not wait for pregnancy or delivery before they begin to pray for their children. There were also two other women on same level playing ground who encountered some trouble. These were Ruth and Orpah - the daughters- in-law of Naomi (Ruth 1). One got it right, the other missed it.

Naomi had followed her husband, Elimelech, to Moab, in search of food. Her husband died and their two sons married two Moabite women, Ruth and Orpah. Her two sons also died leaving her with Ruth and Orpah. In the course of time, she heard that Israel has been visited by God and the famine had receded. Naomi decided to return home. She bade bye to her two daughters in-law. Ruth clung to her mother in law. She decided to go after the woman who came from Israel. She abandoned comfort for the unknown. Listen to her: ***"Where thou diest, will I die, and there will I be buried: the LORD do so to me, and more also, if ought but death part thee and me." Ruth 1:17***

That is the woman of destiny. Today Ruth is mentioned in the genealogy of Jesus (Matthew 1: 5). Meanwhile, Orpah was quick at bidding good bye to her mother-in-law. She lost everything. When we hear such stories, it should ring a bell for us as Christians. Most people will choose comfort and wealth. As such, they are ready to die with any rich man. Young ladies today are following men who can beget them twice and properly be called their grandfathers, because of wealth. Not only are they following their money, they are also following their gods. Many young boys are getting dated to women who qualify to be their grandmothers because such ladies happen to be chief executives of one large firm or the other and they have not been able to get a husband. Many of these women placed themselves in this situation because they had sold their souls to the devil. Many boys are following them to their destruction because of earthly wealth. Young man, young woman look before you leap.

Fast Food Era

We are in the era of fast food when everything must be done fast. Money must be gotten fast. Everything must be fast! fast! fast! The Bible says, "It is the glory of God to conceal a thing: but the honour of kings is to search out a matter" (Proverbs 25:2). Our modern day Christianity says, "God has no right to conceal anything, because there is no time to search." Everything must be bare because time is running out to make money. Yet, time is not running out to go to heaven.

In the early days of the Church when a nation becomes confused young men are sent into monasteries to fast and seek the face of God. That is virtually not the vogue today. Men are interested in being known and as such what is in vogue is television ministry. Power must be advertised because it is the best way to demonstrate power and attract the onlookers. Fasting is too much trouble especially if it is not geared towards acquiring one level of power with the consequent fame and money. Even after a crusade, one will hear words such as, "God moved but it was because we fasted." We try to create God in our image. Each power is to destroy one level of trouble or the other even if the trouble is an arrangement by heaven for our spiritual growth.

God is on the Throne

'In the world you will have trouble', was directed at the followers of Jesus. God did not promise Christians that they are exempted from trouble. In fact, any man who does not want to have this trouble cannot follow Christ. God himself said, "See, I have refined you, though not as silver; I have tested you in the furnace of affliction" (Isaiah 48:10). No matter the extent of the trouble, it behoves the Christian to know that God is on the throne and in control. Our portions are basically two. First we must realise that God is with us. When Moses died, God came to Joshua and said to him, "No one will be able to stand against you all the days of your life. As I was with Moses, so I will be with you; I will never leave you nor forsake you"

(Joshua 1: 5-6). The major problem with us is that we never realise that God is actually with us as He has said. As a result of this lack of realisation, we keep running up and down. The New Living Translation of the Bible puts Jesus words to His disciples more succinctly, "Teach these new disciples to obey all the commands I have given you. **And be sure of this:** I am with you always, even to the end of the age" (Matthew 28: 20). This assurance is critical for this generation. No matter what befalls the world, simply **be sure** that God is with us. It may be a costly assumption to say that he is with you when you are not sure. Thus it also behoves us to have right standing with God for us to be sure that God is with us.

Many people will prefer their brothers, sisters and friends who occupy plum government positions whether they are Christians or not. If your relative or friend is not a Christian, he is as dangerous as Satan because your light is a threat to him. Physically he looks innocuous but spiritually he is against you whether he knows it or not. There are witches who have eaten their children because they might not even "know."

The second portion of the Christian is to be courageous in the face of trouble. God said to Joshua, "Be strong and courageous" (Joshua 1: 6). In our generation it is strong and courageous Christians that will make it to the end. It is those who endure to the end that will be saved. It takes courage to confront the corrupt men in our society. It takes courage to confront the occultic and wicked men of our generation. Instead they are given the front seats in our churches. Like Saul of old, they are making them as special guests as Agag was in the house of Saul, when God has earmarked them for destruction. God is looking for the Samuels who will come and destroy these Agags in our generation.

"And he took Agag the king of the Amalekites alive, and utterly destroyed all the people with the edge of the sword. Then said Samuel, Bring ye hither to me Agag the king of the Amalekites. And Agag came unto him delicately. And Agag said, Surely the bitterness of death is past. And Samuel said, As thy sword hath made women childless, so shall thy mother be childless among women. And Samuel hewed Agag in pieces before the LORD in Gilgal." 1 Samuel 15: 8, 32, 33.

Do you know Satan will try to occupy when the children of God are not courageous. Look at what Agag said above! *And Agag said, "Surely the bitterness of death is past."* Satan knows he is defeated but it is hungry and defeated Christians that are going after all their money and are giving them all the chances in our churches. The true word of God that will destroy satanic kingdoms are never preached. Afterall, all it takes to occupy any plum position in the Church and in the society is money. Our prayer during these trying years is that God will give us men who are courageous to confront the satanic agents of our time. We are soldiers of the Lord. A true soldier dies at his duty post.

Why Does God Allow Suffering?

In this generation, we live in a suffering world where only evil happenings make good news. In fact, it even seems that people are happy listening to such news. A man is killed by his wife, and it is carried in the news. Boko Haram attacks a village and it becomes a major headline. A plane goes missing and it becomes headline news for weeks or even months. The only thing competing with evil news nowadays may be sports news that may help some people to forget their sorrow.

On the other hand, many people in our generation see suffering as a taboo. People see suffering as due to sin or even the devil. We do know that all evil comes from the evil one – the devil. The devil, however, acts as the police. They only punish when one commits crime or breaks the law. Even when one is innocent, he can only be mistakenly punished if government allows it due to ignorance. For God He is never ignorant but could allow suffering. No suffering comes to the child of God without His knowledge. The devils punishes when one disobeys God. God may also allow suffering to come to His children for them to be "made."

Follow me

This is usually the words Jesus used when He called His disciples. "Follow me and I will make you fishers of men." Making takes a process. It took Jesus three good years to make His disciples. In the digital age, we want everything now, now! If it does not happen now, then our time is being wasted. The Bible says that in the furnace of affliction God selects His own (Isaiah 48: 10).

In the book of Judges (Judges 3: 1-3), God said He allowed some of the Canaanite tribes to live among His children – the Israelites, to teach them to war. Most of the children of Israel who were born during the transition from Egypt to the Promised Land had not learnt the art of war. In the same way, God allows suffering among His children to teach them the art of war. When there was war, the Israelites would remember God. In the absence of war, they would relapse into sin. Without suffering, many Christians will never remember God. That is why Jesus said the children of this world are more shrewd (cunny) than the children of the kingdom. They always remember their gods. They prepare ahead for the worst. How many people will go into public service without first visiting a "dibia"? How many are in business without the support of a juju man? Many of them have their personal "attamas." How many become politicians without first of all visiting one big fetish man or the other. In fact, some have churches in the palour but what keeps them in power is one power from the underworld. It is Christians who are careless and they pay dearly for it. They do not allow themselves to have a genuine encounter with God before going to public offices or even business. When a man has a genuine encounter with God, suffering will only plant his feet on a higher ground. Such a man will be a terror to the kingdom of darkness. If he attends any meeting, be it business or political, he dictates the tunes of the happening. His word is like the word of God to his hearers, just like the word of Moses was to his generation. Generally, it is the word of the occultic people that usually hold sway in our generation because Christians are generally not very serious. Before such Christians will attend any meeting, they would have swallowed "something," or even when making contribution to any debate, there is a fetish kola nut on their tongue. In fact, these days Christians even go to such people for guidance and counselling!

The Cross and Suffering
These days it is common to hear people talking about how they are carrying their crosses. A man that is being troubled by the wife will say, "I am carrying my cross", and vice versa. A man being troubled by his bad-mannered child will say, "I am carrying my cross." A man suffering from a chronic illness will say, "I am carrying my cross." The cross is not equivalent to suffering per se. There is element of suffering in the cross but that is not what it typifies. A man carrying his cross in the era

of Jesus would mean there is a life to be destroyed. It typified death. That of Jesus which most Christians refer to means that there is something to be destroyed to improve the lot of others. When Jesus went to the cross, He carried the sin of humanity there to nail the nature of sin on the cross. Anyone who says that he is carrying his cross, the first question is, "What are you going to nail on it." The cross is for crucifying self that will not allow you to encounter God genuinely. As such your ego is always in the fore. Someone said, ego means, Edging God Out. That your bad habit of womanising can only be destroyed on the crossing. That your bad habit of alcoholism can only be destroyed on the cross. The list can continue. The cross is for a temporary suffering that will be bring a permanent glory. Suffering because of sin is not a cross. In fact, sickness that does not bring your closer to God is not a cross. There is a glory beyond the cross. There is a glory beyond that suffering that will make you into what God wants you to be. Remember God is the master potter. Every pot must pass through the fire to give it the strength it needs to pass through the usage it is meant for.

The Pains And Gains Of Disappointment

Michael Adikwu

The Pains And Gains Of Disappointment

www.ingramcontent.com/pod-product-compliance
Lightning Source LLC
Chambersburg PA
CBHW052112110526
44592CB00013B/1573